# December

Week 53

 MW00898828

12/28/20 - 01/03/21

○ 28. MONDAY

PRIORITIES

_____

_____

○ 29. TUESDAY

_____

_____

_____

_____

_____

○ 30. WEDNESDAY

TO DO

_____

_____

○ 31. THURSDAY

_____

_____

_____

_____

_____

○ 1. FRIDAY

_____

_____

_____

_____

○ 2. SATURDAY / 3. SUNDAY

_____

_____

_____

_____

# January

Week 1                                        01/04/21 - 01/10/21

---

○ 4. MONDAY

PRIORITIES

_____
_____
_____
_____
○ 5. TUESDAY
_____
_____
_____
_____

○ 6. WEDNESDAY

TO DO

_____
_____
_____
_____
○ 7. THURSDAY
_____
_____
_____
_____
○ 8. FRIDAY
_____
_____
_____
_____
○ 9. SATURDAY / 10. SUNDAY
_____
_____
_____
_____

# January

Week 2                                      01/11/21 - 01/17/21

○ 11. MONDAY

**PRIORITIES**

○ 12. TUESDAY

○ 13. WEDNESDAY

**TO DO**

○ 14. THURSDAY

○ 15. FRIDAY

○ 16. SATURDAY / 17. SUNDAY

# January

Week 3                                          01/18/21 - 01/24/21

---

○ 18. MONDAY

**PRIORITIES**

○ 19. TUESDAY

○ 20. WEDNESDAY

**TO DO**

○ 21. THURSDAY

○ 22. FRIDAY

○ 23. SATURDAY / 24. SUNDAY

# January

○ 25. MONDAY

PRIORITIES

○ 26. TUESDAY

○ 27. WEDNESDAY

TO DO

○ 28. THURSDAY

○ 29. FRIDAY

○ 30. SATURDAY / 31. SUNDAY

# February

Week 5

---

○ 1. MONDAY

PRIORITIES

_____
_____
_____
_____
_____
_____

○ 2. TUESDAY

---

○ 3. WEDNESDAY

TO DO

_____
_____
_____
_____
_____
_____

○ 4. THURSDAY

_____
_____
_____
_____

○ 5. FRIDAY

_____
_____
_____

○ 6. SATURDAY / 7. SUNDAY

_____
_____

# February

○ 8. MONDAY

**PRIORITIES**

○ 9. TUESDAY

○ 10. WEDNESDAY

**TO DO**

○ 11. THURSDAY

○ 12. FRIDAY

○ 13. SATURDAY / 14. SUNDAY

# February

Week 7                                                02/15/21 - 02/21/21

○ 15. MONDAY

PRIORITIES

○ 16. TUESDAY

○ 17. WEDNESDAY

TO DO

○ 18. THURSDAY

○ 19. FRIDAY

○ 20. SATURDAY / 21. SUNDAY

# February

○ 22. MONDAY

**PRIORITIES**

○ 23. TUESDAY

○ 24. WEDNESDAY

**TO DO**

○ 25. THURSDAY

○ 26. FRIDAY

○ 27. SATURDAY / 28. SUNDAY

# March

Week 9                                        03/01/21 - 03/07/21

---

○ 1. MONDAY

PRIORITIES

_____

○ 2. TUESDAY

_____

○ 3. WEDNESDAY

TO DO

_____

○ 4. THURSDAY

_____

○ 5. FRIDAY

_____

○ 6. SATURDAY / 7. SUNDAY

# March

○ 8. MONDAY

PRIORITIES

○ 9. TUESDAY

○ 10. WEDNESDAY

TO DO

○ 11. THURSDAY

○ 12. FRIDAY

○ 13. SATURDAY / 14. SUNDAY

# March

---

○ 15. MONDAY

PRIORITIES

_____

_____

_____

_____

_____

○ 16. TUESDAY

_____

_____

_____

_____

○ 17. WEDNESDAY

TO DO

_____

_____

_____

○ 18. THURSDAY

_____

_____

_____

_____

○ 19. FRIDAY

_____

_____

_____

_____

_____

○ 20. SATURDAY / 21. SUNDAY

_____

_____

_____

_____

_____

# March

Week 12                                   03/22/21 - 03/28/21

---

○ 22. MONDAY

_____

_____

_____

○ 23. TUESDAY

_____

_____

_____

_____

○ 24. WEDNESDAY

TO DO

_____

_____

○ 25. THURSDAY

_____

_____

_____

_____

○ 26. FRIDAY

_____

_____

_____

_____

○ 27. SATURDAY / 28. SUNDAY

_____

_____

_____

_____

# March

Week 13

---

○ 29. MONDAY

PRIORITIES

○ 30. TUESDAY

○ 31. WEDNESDAY

TO DO

○ 1. THURSDAY

○ 2. FRIDAY

○ 3. SATURDAY / 4. SUNDAY

# April

04/05/21 - 04/11/21

○ 5. MONDAY

PRIORITIES

○ 6. TUESDAY

○ 7. WEDNESDAY

TO DO

○ 8. THURSDAY

○ 9. FRIDAY

○ 10. SATURDAY / 11. SUNDAY

# April

Week 15                                    04/12/21 - 04/18/21

---

◯ 12. MONDAY

PRIORITIES

_____
_____
_____
_____

◯ 13. TUESDAY

_____
_____
_____
_____

---

◯ 14. WEDNESDAY

TO DO

_____
_____
_____
_____

◯ 15. THURSDAY

_____
_____
_____
_____

---

◯ 16. FRIDAY

_____
_____
_____
_____
_____

◯ 17. SATURDAY / 18. SUNDAY

_____
_____
_____
_____

# April

04/19/21 - 04/25/21

○ 19. MONDAY

PRIORITIES

○ 20. TUESDAY

○ 21. WEDNESDAY

TO DO

○ 22. THURSDAY

○ 23. FRIDAY

○ 24. SATURDAY / 25. SUNDAY

# April

Week 17                                          04/26/21 - 05/02/21

○ 26. MONDAY

PRIORITIES

○ 27. TUESDAY

○ 28. WEDNESDAY

TO DO

○ 29. THURSDAY

○ 30. FRIDAY

○ 1. SATURDAY / 2. SUNDAY

# May

○ 3. MONDAY

**PRIORITIES**

○ 4. TUESDAY

○ 5. WEDNESDAY

**TO DO**

○ 6. THURSDAY

○ 7. FRIDAY

○ 8. SATURDAY / 9. SUNDAY

# May

Week 19                                    05/10/21 - 05/16/21

---

○ 10. MONDAY

PRIORITIES

_____

_____

_____

_____

_____

○ 11. TUESDAY

_____

_____

_____

_____

○ 12. WEDNESDAY

TO DO

_____

_____

_____

○ 13. THURSDAY

_____

_____

_____

_____

_____

○ 14. FRIDAY

_____

_____

_____

_____

_____

○ 15. SATURDAY / 16. SUNDAY

_____

_____

_____

_____

_____

# May

05/17/21 - 05/23/21

○ 17. MONDAY

PRIORITIES

○ 18. TUESDAY

○ 19. WEDNESDAY

TO DO

○ 20. THURSDAY

○ 21. FRIDAY

○ 22. SATURDAY / 23. SUNDAY

# May

○ 24. MONDAY

PRIORITIES

○ 25. TUESDAY

○ 26. WEDNESDAY

TO DO

○ 27. THURSDAY

○ 28. FRIDAY

○ 29. SATURDAY / 30. SUNDAY

# May

○ 31. MONDAY

PRIORITIES

○ 1. TUESDAY

○ 2. WEDNESDAY

TO DO

○ 3. THURSDAY

○ 4. FRIDAY

○ 5. SATURDAY / 6. SUNDAY

# June

Week 23                                  06/07/21 - 06/13/21

---

○ 7. MONDAY

PRIORITIES

---

○ 8. TUESDAY

---

○ 9. WEDNESDAY

TO DO

---

○ 10. THURSDAY

---

○ 11. FRIDAY

---

○ 12. SATURDAY / 13. SUNDAY

# June

Week 24 06/14/21 - 06/20/21

○ 14. MONDAY

○ 15. TUESDAY

○ 16. WEDNESDAY

○ 17. THURSDAY

○ 18. FRIDAY

○ 19. SATURDAY / 20. SUNDAY

PRIORITIES

TO DO

# June

○ 21. MONDAY

PRIORITIES

○ 22. TUESDAY

○ 23. WEDNESDAY

TO DO

○ 24. THURSDAY

○ 25. FRIDAY

○ 26. SATURDAY / 27. SUNDAY

# June

Week 26

○ 28. MONDAY

PRIORITIES

○ 29. TUESDAY

○ 30. WEDNESDAY

TO DO

○ 1. THURSDAY

○ 2. FRIDAY

○ 3. SATURDAY / 4. SUNDAY

# July

07/05/21 - 07/11/21

---

○ 5. MONDAY

PRIORITIES

○ 6. TUESDAY

○ 7. WEDNESDAY

TO DO

○ 8. THURSDAY

○ 9. FRIDAY

○ 10. SATURDAY / 11. SUNDAY

# July

Week 28

○ 12. MONDAY

PRIORITIES

○ 13. TUESDAY

○ 14. WEDNESDAY

TO DO

○ 15. THURSDAY

○ 16. FRIDAY

○ 17. SATURDAY / 18. SUNDAY

# July

○ 19. MONDAY

PRIORITIES

○ 20. TUESDAY

○ 21. WEDNESDAY

TO DO

○ 22. THURSDAY

○ 23. FRIDAY

○ 24. SATURDAY / 25. SUNDAY

# July

07/26/21 - 08/01/21

○ 26. MONDAY

**PRIORITIES**

○ 27. TUESDAY

○ 28. WEDNESDAY

**TO DO**

○ 29. THURSDAY

○ 30. FRIDAY

○ 31. SATURDAY / 1. SUNDAY

# August

Week 31                                     08/02/21 - 08/08/21

○ 2. MONDAY

PRIORITIES

○ 3. TUESDAY

○ 4. WEDNESDAY

TO DO

○ 5. THURSDAY

○ 6. FRIDAY

○ 7. SATURDAY / 8. SUNDAY

# August

Week 32

08/09/21 - 08/15/21

---

○ 9. MONDAY

**PRIORITIES**

 

 

 

○ 10. TUESDAY

 

 

 

○ 11. WEDNESDAY

**TO DO**

 

 

○ 12. THURSDAY

 

 

 

○ 13. FRIDAY

 

 

 

○ 14. SATURDAY / 15. SUNDAY

 

 

 

# August

○ 16. MONDAY

PRIORITIES

○ 17. TUESDAY

○ 18. WEDNESDAY

TO DO

○ 19. THURSDAY

○ 20. FRIDAY

○ 21. SATURDAY / 22. SUNDAY

# August

○ 23. MONDAY

PRIORITIES

○ 24. TUESDAY

○ 25. WEDNESDAY

TO DO

○ 26. THURSDAY

○ 27. FRIDAY

○ 28. SATURDAY / 29. SUNDAY

# August

Week 35                                    08/30/21 - 09/05/21

○ 30. MONDAY

PRIORITIES

○ 31. TUESDAY

○ 1. WEDNESDAY

TO DO

○ 2. THURSDAY

○ 3. FRIDAY

○ 4. SATURDAY / 5. SUNDAY

# September

09/06/21 - 09/12/21

○ 6. MONDAY

PRIORITIES

○ 7. TUESDAY

○ 8. WEDNESDAY

TO DO

○ 9. THURSDAY

○ 10. FRIDAY

○ 11. SATURDAY / 12. SUNDAY

# September

○ 13. MONDAY

PRIORITIES

○ 14. TUESDAY

○ 15. WEDNESDAY

TO DO

○ 16. THURSDAY

○ 17. FRIDAY

○ 18. SATURDAY / 19. SUNDAY

# September

09/20/21 - 09/26/21

---

○ 20. MONDAY

PRIORITIES

---

○ 21. TUESDAY

---

○ 22. WEDNESDAY

TO DO

---

○ 23. THURSDAY

---

○ 24. FRIDAY

---

○ 25. SATURDAY / 26. SUNDAY

# September

Week 39                                    09/27/21 - 10/03/21

○ 27. MONDAY

PRIORITIES

○ 28. TUESDAY

○ 29. WEDNESDAY

TO DO

○ 30. THURSDAY

○ 1. FRIDAY

○ 2. SATURDAY / 3. SUNDAY

# October

Week 40

○ 4. MONDAY

PRIORITIES

○ 5. TUESDAY

○ 6. WEDNESDAY

TO DO

○ 7. THURSDAY

○ 8. FRIDAY

○ 9. SATURDAY / 10. SUNDAY

# October

---

○ 11. MONDAY

PRIORITIES

---

○ 12. TUESDAY

---

○ 13. WEDNESDAY

TO DO

---

○ 14. THURSDAY

---

○ 15. FRIDAY

---

○ 16. SATURDAY / 17. SUNDAY

# October

○ 18. MONDAY

PRIORITIES

○ 19. TUESDAY

○ 20. WEDNESDAY

TO DO

○ 21. THURSDAY

○ 22. FRIDAY

○ 23. SATURDAY / 24. SUNDAY

# October

○ 25. MONDAY

PRIORITIES

○ 26. TUESDAY

○ 27. WEDNESDAY

TO DO

○ 28. THURSDAY

○ 29. FRIDAY

○ 30. SATURDAY / 31. SUNDAY

# November

11/01/21 - 11/07/21

○ 1. MONDAY

**PRIORITIES**

○ 2. TUESDAY

○ 3. WEDNESDAY

**TO DO**

○ 4. THURSDAY

○ 5. FRIDAY

○ 6. SATURDAY / 7. SUNDAY

# November

Week 45

11/08/21 - 11/14/21

○ 8. MONDAY

PRIORITIES

○ 9. TUESDAY

○ 10. WEDNESDAY

TO DO

○ 11. THURSDAY

○ 12. FRIDAY

○ 13. SATURDAY / 14. SUNDAY

# November

○ 15. MONDAY

PRIORITIES

○ 16. TUESDAY

○ 17. WEDNESDAY

TO DO

○ 18. THURSDAY

○ 19. FRIDAY

○ 20. SATURDAY / 21. SUNDAY

# November

Week 47                                          11/22/21 - 11/28/21

---

○ 22. MONDAY

PRIORITIES

○ 23. TUESDAY

○ 24. WEDNESDAY

TO DO

○ 25. THURSDAY

○ 26. FRIDAY

○ 27. SATURDAY / 28. SUNDAY

# November

○ 29. MONDAY

**PRIORITIES**

○ 30. TUESDAY

○ 1. WEDNESDAY

**TO DO**

○ 2. THURSDAY

○ 3. FRIDAY

○ 4. SATURDAY / 5. SUNDAY

# December

Week 49                                    12/06/21 - 12/12/21

---

○ 6. MONDAY

PRIORITIES

_____
_____
_____
_____

○ 7. TUESDAY

_____
_____
_____
_____

○ 8. WEDNESDAY

TO DO

_____
_____
_____

○ 9. THURSDAY

_____
_____
_____
_____

○ 10. FRIDAY

_____
_____
_____
_____

○ 11. SATURDAY / 12. SUNDAY

_____
_____
_____
_____

# December

○ 13. MONDAY

PRIORITIES

○ 14. TUESDAY

○ 15. WEDNESDAY

TO DO

○ 16. THURSDAY

○ 17. FRIDAY

○ 18. SATURDAY / 19. SUNDAY

# December

12/20/21 - 12/26/21

---

○ 20. MONDAY

PRIORITIES

_____

_____

○ 21. TUESDAY

_____

_____

_____

_____

○ 22. WEDNESDAY

TO DO

_____

_____

_____

○ 23. THURSDAY

_____

_____

_____

_____

○ 24. FRIDAY

_____

_____

_____

_____

○ 25. SATURDAY / 26. SUNDAY

_____

_____

_____

_____

# December

Week 52                                    12/27/21 - 01/02/22

○ 27. MONDAY

                                           PRIORITIES

○ 28. TUESDAY

○ 29. WEDNESDAY

                                           TO DO

○ 30. THURSDAY

○ 31. FRIDAY

○ 1. SATURDAY / 2. SUNDAY

Made in the USA
Monee, IL
11 September 2021